With gratitude to the members of the
Children's Visionary Circle and all of the
extraordinary donors who helped to make
Ann & Robert H. Lurie Children's
Hospital of Chicago a reality.

February 25, 2014

Ann & Robert H. Lurie
Children's Hospital of Chicago™

Bruce King Komiske, MHA, FACHE

Editor

images
Publishing

Published in Australia in 2013 by
The Images Publishing Group Pty Ltd
ABN 89 059 734 431
6 Bastow Place, Mulgrave, Victoria 3170, Australia
Tel: +61 3 9561 5544 Fax: +61 3 9561 4860
books@imagespublishing.com
www.imagespublishing.com

Copyright © The Images Publishing Group Pty Ltd 2013
The Images Publishing Group Reference Number: 1048

National Library of Australia Cataloguing-in-Publication entry:

Author:	Komiske, Bruce.
Title:	Ann & Robert H. Lurie Children's Hospital of Chicago / Bruce Komiske
ISBN:	9781864705218 (hbk.)
Subjects:	Ann & Robert H. Lurie Children's Hospital of Chicago.
	Children—Hospitals—United States—Chicago.
	Hospital architecture—United States—Chicago.
	Hospital buildings—Design and construction.
Dewey number	725.570977311

Edited by Driss Fatih

Designed by The Graphic Image Studio Pty Ltd, Mulgrave, Australia
www.tgis.com.au

Pre-publishing services by United Graphic Pte Ltd, Singapore
Printed by Everbest Printing Co. Ltd in Hong Kong/China on 140 gsm GoldEast Matt Art paper

IMAGES has included on its website a page for special notices in relation to this and our other publications. Please visit www.imagespublishing.com.

*This book is dedicated to all who had a part
in creating Ann & Robert H. Lurie
Children's Hospital of Chicago.*

On behalf of the children and families we are privileged to serve,
I want to extend a heartfelt thanks to everyone involved in the creation
of Ann & Robert H. Lurie Children's Hospital of Chicago. Our goal was
to design a facility that would enable us to enhance our mission of caring
for critically ill and injured children for generations to come.
Together, we achieved this goal.

We now have a hospital building that is worthy of the outstanding
caregivers who share their time and talent with our children each day.
With the continued support and partnership of the greater community,
we look forward to elevating children's healthcare to new heights.

Patrick M. Magoon
President and CEO

Contents

Legacy of Hope and Healing

In the years following the Great Chicago Fire of 1871, Chicago was a booming metropolis and one of the fastest-growing cities in the world. As America's railroad hub and "hog butcher to the world"—a phrase coined by writer Carl Sandburg—Chicago was the link between the vast, fertile lands of the west and the populated cities of the east. Although the city prospered and grew, the prognosis for children born in the city in those days was grim. A child had only a 50 percent chance of surviving to the age of five, and those who survived were likely to be exposed to a host of diseases.

In 1882, a young widow who had tragically lost her young son to a deadly disease took bold steps to transform the future of children's health in Chicago. Renovating a modest home at the corner of Belden and Halsted streets for $13,000, Julia Foster Porter established Chicago's first hospital dedicated exclusively to caring for children. From these modest roots, with the support of many community partners, Julia's cottage would eventually become Children's Memorial Hospital. About a decade later, when demand for its services called for a larger and more modern facility, the hospital moved to a triangle of land in an undeveloped area of Lincoln Park, which would remain the hospital's home for the next 120 years.

Throughout the years, generous families, corporations, and foundations helped to make the hospital the special place it is today. More than 125 years after its founding, the hospital embarked on a bold initiative to build Ann & Robert H. Lurie Children's Hospital of Chicago. Just like Julia's original cottage in 1882, this state-of-the-art facility serves as an agent of change, shaping pediatric health care in Chicago and beyond.

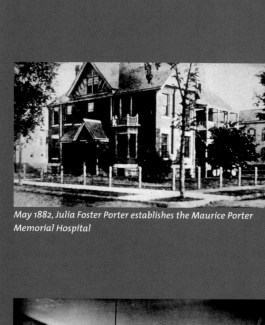
May 1882, Julia Foster Porter establishes the Maurice Porter Memorial Hospital

Infirmary 1907

Outdoor gathering

HOSPITAL GROUNDS ABOUT 1913

Laying the foundations of the new wing 1930

Main building from street 1924

Extension 1928

The Children's Memorial Hospital—Yesterday and Today
1. Thomas D. Jones Memorial, 2. Martha Wilson Memorial, 3. Maurice
Porter Memorial, 4. Agnes Wilson Memorial, 5. and 6. K. Building, 7. Service Shop, 8. Power Plant and Laundry, 9. Nellie A. Black Memorial, 10.
James Deering Memorial, 11. Employees' Residence

The Planning and Design Process

The planning and design of Lurie Children's was an 8-year process that included top architects, more than 800 physicians and staff members, Chicago's top cultural institutions, and most importantly, the kids and families served by the hospital.

Following the Children's Memorial Hospital Board of Directors resolution to plan for the relocation of its existing hospital in 2004, hospital staff formed user groups to work with Kurt Salmon Associates to develop the programming for a new hospital. In 2006, the downtown site on the campus of Northwestern University Feinberg School of Medicine was chosen and architects from Zimmer Gunsul Frasca, Solomon Cordwell Buenz and Anderson Mikos began converting this work into a design. Their charge was to fit all the necessary elements of a state-of-the-art pediatric medical center on the site while continuing to reinforce the hospital's top priority: family-centered care. To ensure that these values were fully integrated into the design, project leaders engaged the hospital's Family Advisory Board and Kids' Advisory Board. These parents and teenagers, who have spent significant time at the hospital, shared valuable insight about life in the hospital from a child and family member's perspective. They advocated for a healing, optimistic environment that accommodates the range of emotions that are experienced during a hospital stay. They made the case for the importance of respite and home-like spaces.

Once the preliminary interior design was done, mock-up rooms were created so that staff could do simulations and recommend changes as needed. A mock-up room was also created in the hospital's main lobby and a nearby computer enabled families and visitors to share their impressions of the new design and provide feedback.

The exterior design presented a unique challenge because the top half of the building, primarily inpatient units, was larger than the bottom half. Several exterior design ideas were created and vetted by the Board, community leaders, staff, and families. The final design was a sophisticated but child-like play on building blocks. It includes unique elements such as specialty windows and the hospital's treasured "hand" logo to reinforce the unique care being delivered inside the building.

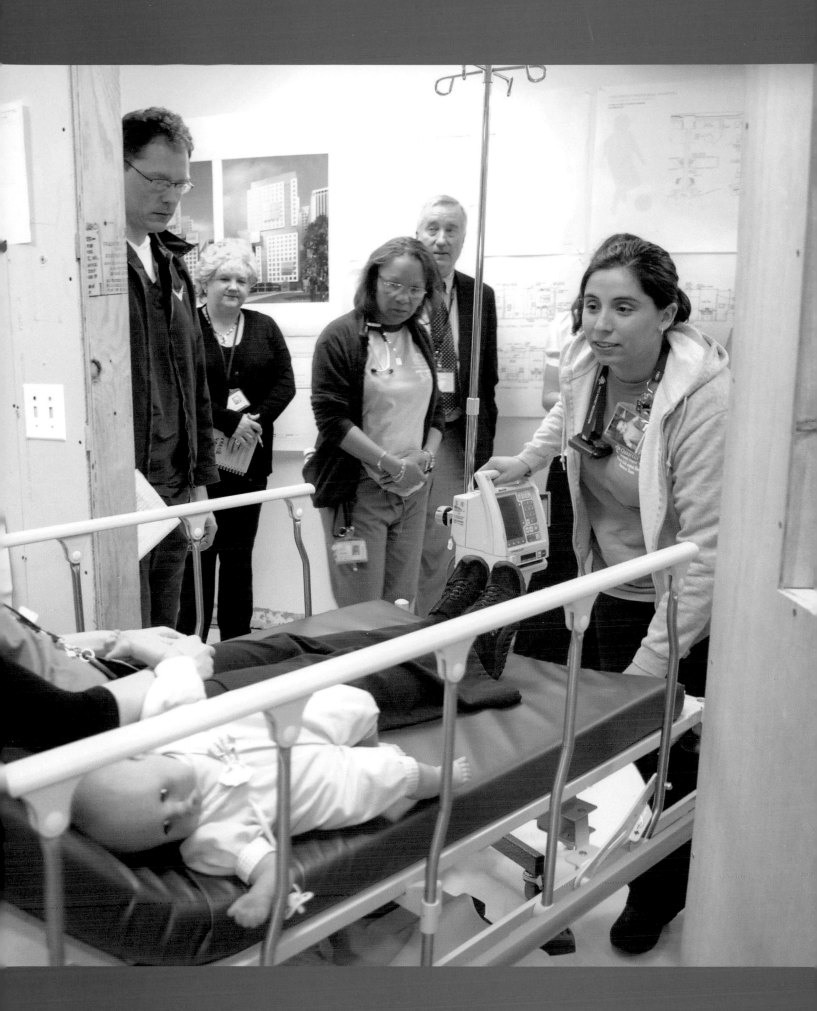

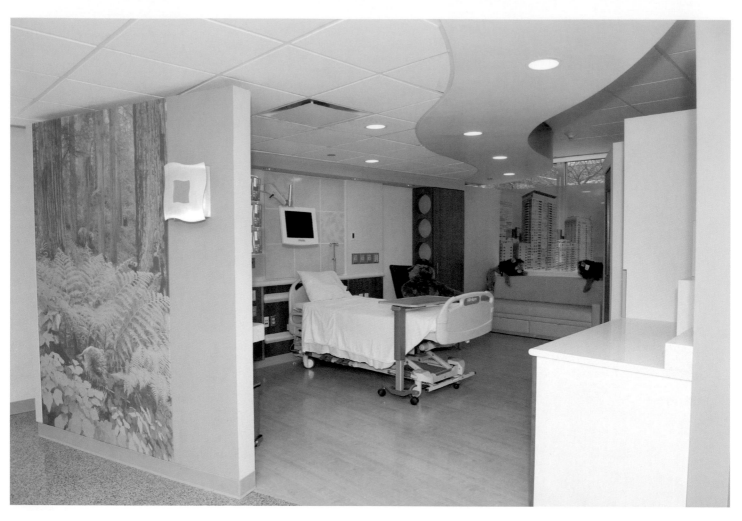

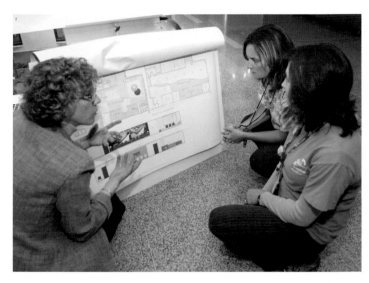

Evolution of
exterior design

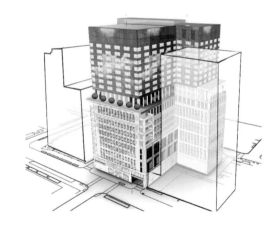

Construction 2008–2012

10,000 pounds of steel. 1,792 precast exterior panels. 3,573 doors. 921 windows.

Building the tallest children's hospital in the world on a 1.8-acre site was no small project. The two giant red tower cranes, named Hope and Courage in an employee contest, became the hospital's first visible presence on its new site. But long before the cranes arrived, the construction management team, Mortenson Power, had begun their planning. They knew that the key to success would be team coordination and a commitment to safety.

The site was small, the area was full of vehicle and pedestrian traffic, and the nearby hospital and university operations could not be disrupted. Efficient scheduling, routing, and unloading were essential, and were implemented using a "just in time" delivery program.

The creation of a digital prototype and use of Building Information Modeling (BIM) tools and process enabled the entire team to work together and blurred the traditional boundaries between designers and builders. Potential issues were caught and resolved on computer screens well before subcontractors even began work in some areas.

Safety was of paramount importance. The Mortenson Power team implemented a comprehensive program that included intense training, observations, and daily meetings about safety-related activities. The project's safety record was impeccable and exceeded all goals and expectations.

The hospital was proud to surpass by more than 20 percent its voluntary goal of providing at least $100 million in contracting opportunity to women- and minority-owned businesses.

Thousands of tradespeople and construction workers came together over the course of four years to build Lurie Children's.

16

Self-climbing core form

Patrick G. and Shirley W. Ryan

Crown and Goodman
Families

Ann Lurie

Bend and Stretch

Bend and Stretch exercises are a long-time tradition in construction safety. Crews start the day in a group bend and stretch with a goal of eliminating workplace accidents and injuries. It also fosters safety, sport, and solidarity.

In 2010, the first patient from Children's Memorial visited the new construction site as a guest leader of Bend and Stretch. Each child prepared a short exercise to music performed from a platform constructed by the crew, complete with speakers and sound system.

There were many motivating moments...Aaron, 11, a spina bifida patient, carefully negotiating his way on crutches to the middle of the platform, looked out at the hundreds of workers, and, with a deep breath and his trademark grin, cued the sound guy, "Hit it!," dropped his crutches and began; 14-year-old triplets Corbin, Jackson, and Spencer, born with varying degrees of cerebral palsy, one confined to a wheelchair, proudly announcing to the crew that each had obtained black belts in martial arts; Jam, teaching the crew boxing moves she had used to stay strong while she fought cancer twice, "I kicked cancer's butt, I'm 11 and I'm cancer-free;" and Drew , 3½, diagnosed with stage IV neuroblastoma at 2 years old and who underwent surgery, chemotherapy, radiation, and a stem cell transplant, taking the hand of his grandfather, a sheet metal foreman working on Lurie Children's site. Surrounded by cheering co-workers, they led the Bend and Stretch side by side.

The visits were so popular that they became a regular event and were covered by local and national media, bringing visibility to both the project and its mission. Posters of kids leading workers appeared on floors and in elevators and became banners for safety events.

In 2011, many of the children who had led Bend and Stretch over the past two years gathered together in a final team exercise. It was their opportunity to say thank you to the dedicated construction workers who would deliver a world-class hospital safely, on time, and under budget.

What should workers wear at the jobsite?

Isabella - Age 5

Do the workers always have to wear a hard hat?

Madeline - Age 3

Why do you think workers need to be safe?

Mikey - Age 5

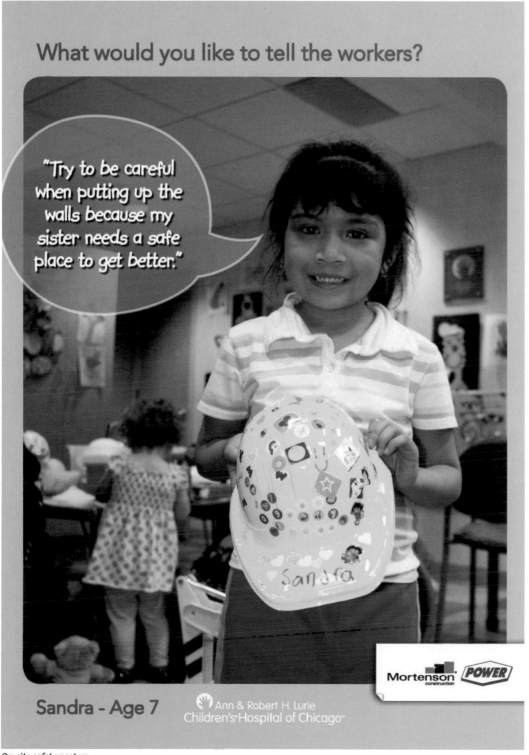

On-site safety posters

Garden in the Sky

The centerpiece of Lurie Children's commitment to healing spaces is the Crown Sky Garden on the 11th floor of the hospital. The space, named in honor of the Crown Family, subtly divides the 5,000-square-foot garden into zones. Areas closer to the Sky Café are designed for high activity and performances, while areas closer to the windows encourage quiet activity and respite for families and staff.

World-renowned landscape architect Mikyoung Kim worked closely with a group of Chicago civic leaders, philanthropists, and volunteers, including visionary leadership from Paula Crown. She also engaged the hospital's patient care leadership, design and construction team, Kids' Advisory Board, and Family Advisory Board in the process.

Measuring the Impact of Design on Healing

There are significant gaps in what is known about the role of respite and play spaces in children's hospitals in a patient's health and healing. Quantification of hospital design has applicability nationwide with the growing interest in building new healing spaces for children. The generosity and foresight of the Crown Family in creating the Crown Sky Garden, a place of respite for patients and their families, presents a unique opportunity to advance the knowledge of the connection between hospital design and health.

An expert, multi-disciplinary research team at Lurie Children's is partnering with the internationally recognized Center for Health Design to examine the impact of hospital design on stress levels in hospitalized children and their parents. The study will explore the extent to which healing spaces promote health and healing during hospitalization. Findings will measure how the Crown Sky Garden, and other spaces, support Lurie Children's efforts to provide a true healing environment for families.

Mikyoung Kim with civic leaders (top) and hospital patients from Kids' Advisory Board (above)

Lester and Renée Crown with James S. and Paula H. Crown

Benches created from trees planted by Frederic Law Olmsted for the Columbian Exposition of 1893

Founders' Board Tree House

Engaging the City of Chicago in the Design Process

I t has been said that Chicago is "the city that works." The creation of Lurie Children's could be evidence that Chicago is actually "the city that works together."

Families, staff, and visitors experience this as they walk through the hospital. Research has shown that lowering children's anxiety in a hospital setting can actually improve outcomes. When hospital leaders began to share this information with the city and ask for help, the response was overwhelming.

More than 20 of the city's top cultural organizations and institutions immediately volunteered to use their expertise to partner with the hospital to create an environment that would help heal children. Donations poured in—life-size whales, a fire truck cab, dinosaur bones, and world-renowned works of art.

The hospital began this process by hosting a design charrette with artists from all of these organizations. It was a day-long brainstorming session about how they could together transform this space to contribute to healing. Given the city's rich cultural diversity, they settled on a theme of "What Makes Chicago Distinctive."

The charrette led to years of work with these cultural partners that resulted in 23 floors of special, child-friendly designs with unique art and interactive exhibits that celebrate the spirit of Chicago.

Design charrette March 2008

Kids' Advisory Board

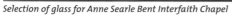
Selection of glass for Anne Searle Bent Interfaith Chapel

Raising of the
Fire Truck

Fire truck cab donated by Pierce Manufacturing, September 2009

Whale sculpture created by Vic Joyner and donated by Shedd Aquarium

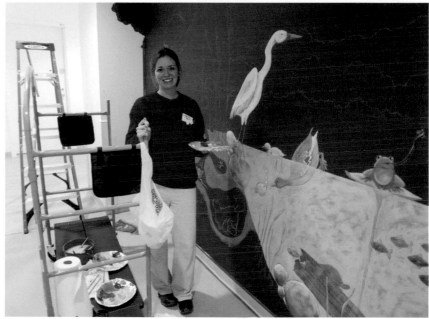

Engaging the City of Chicago in the Design Process

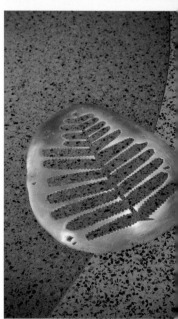

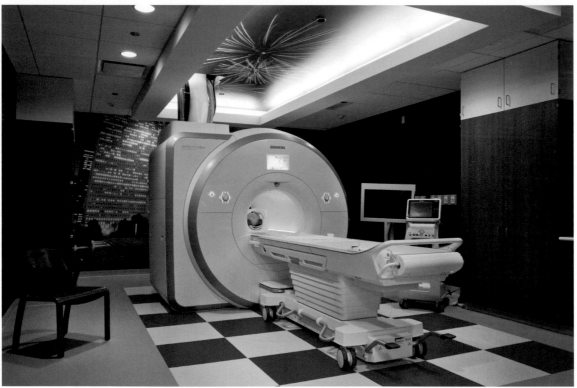

Larry Broutman's "Animals in Chicago" wayfinding photos

78

The Complete Building

Every aspect of the 23-story Ann & Robert H. Lurie Children's Hospital of Chicago was designed with kids in mind. An extraordinary place for healing and family-centered care, the hospital's evidence-based design and advanced technology will enable its outstanding caregivers to provide superior care to the region's most critically ill and injured children.

With a strong commitment to patients, families, staff, and the community, Lurie Children's created a hospital environment that conserves energy, reduces water consumption, uses renewable resources, and recycles waste. The hospital will be a Leadership in Energy and Environmental Design (LEED®) Gold Certified facility and will serve as a role model for sustainable and high-performance design.

The hospital includes 288 inpatient beds in all private rooms, multiple sub-specialty outpatient clinics, a three-floor interventional/procedural platform, emergency department, and the latest diagnostic imaging services.

Inpatient beds are located on the upper floors to maximize privacy, security, daylight, and views of the city. Also, the building was designed to ensure quieter patient and family areas. To accomplish this, "on-stage" corridors run along the face of patient rooms, while "back-stage" corridors allow staff access to support spaces away from families.

The hospital's public and family support spaces are located on the 11th and 12th floors. These areas house the Crown Sky Garden, a cafeteria, gift shop, conference center, chapel, family life center, and sleep suites.

Great attention was given to which colors are utilized in each area of the hospital. Color selections for the hospital are based on five palettes—city, park, lake, woods, and prairie—inspired by Chicago and the surrounding regions. The colors and themes also contribute to wayfinding between and throughout the floors of the hospital. When these colors come together with the creative installations from more than 20 of Chicago's cultural organizations and institutions, the hospital's environment educates, engages, and contributes to the healing process for patients and families.

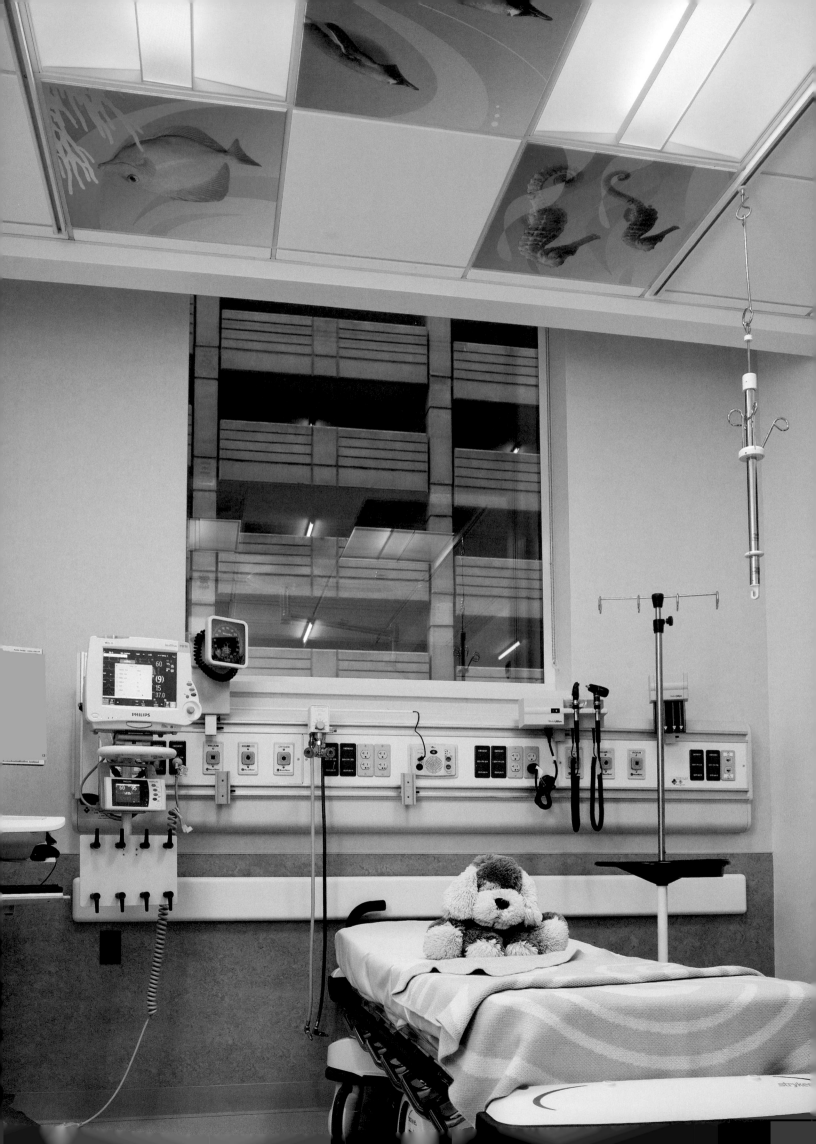

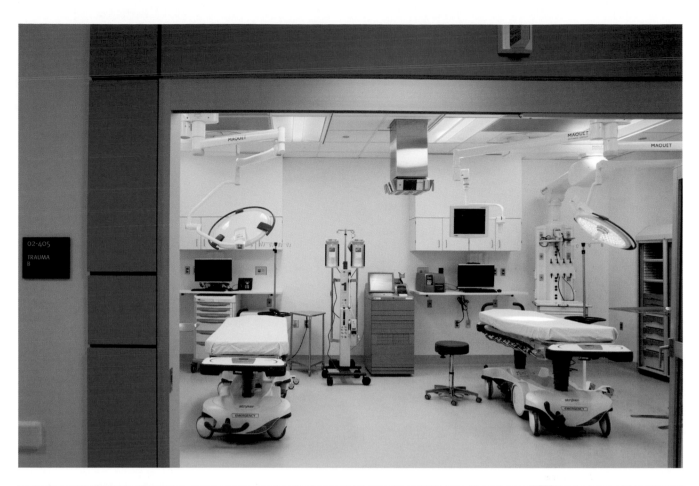

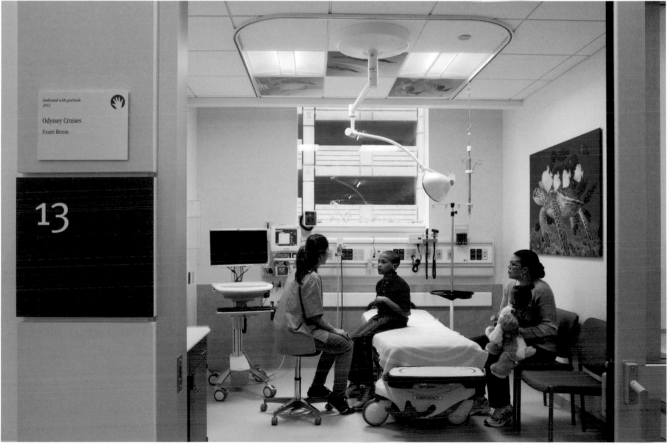

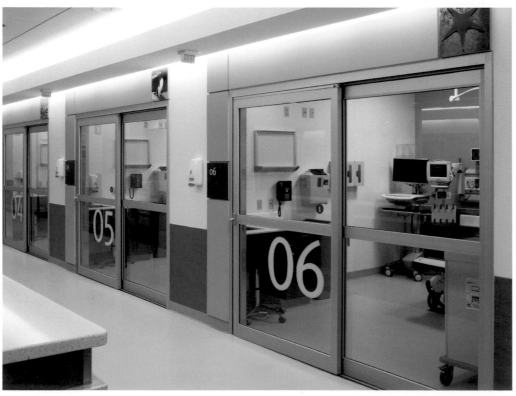

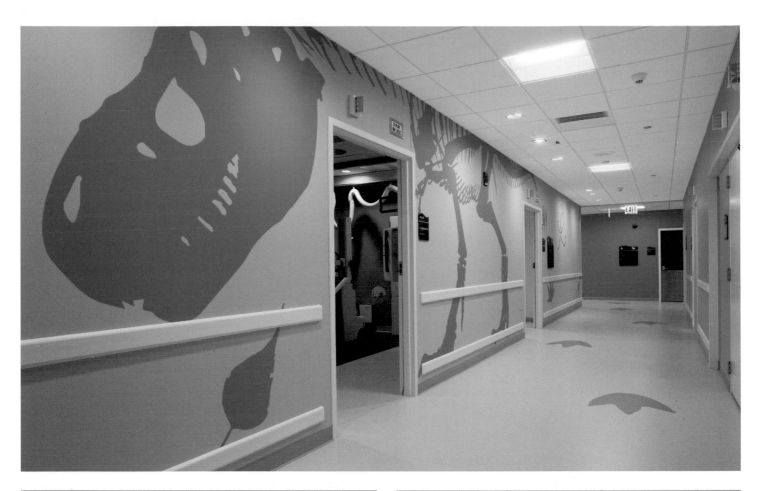

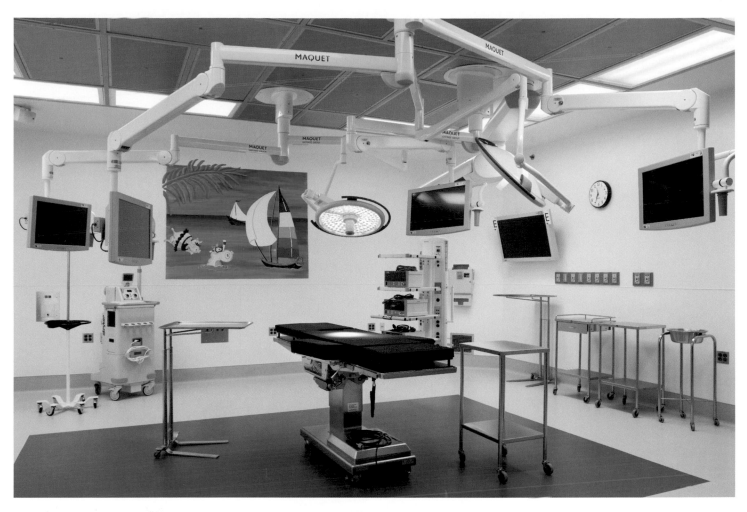

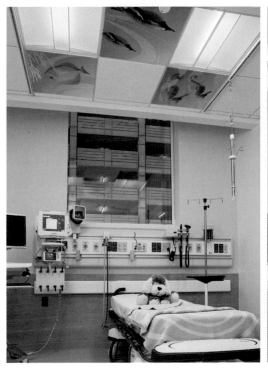

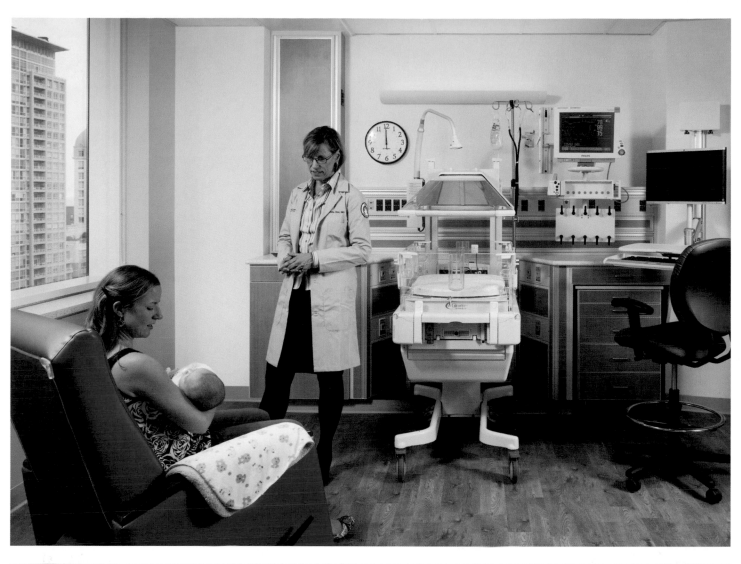

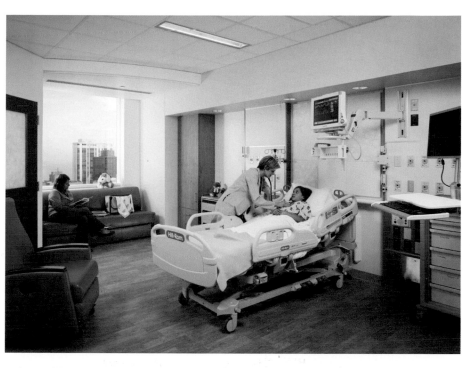

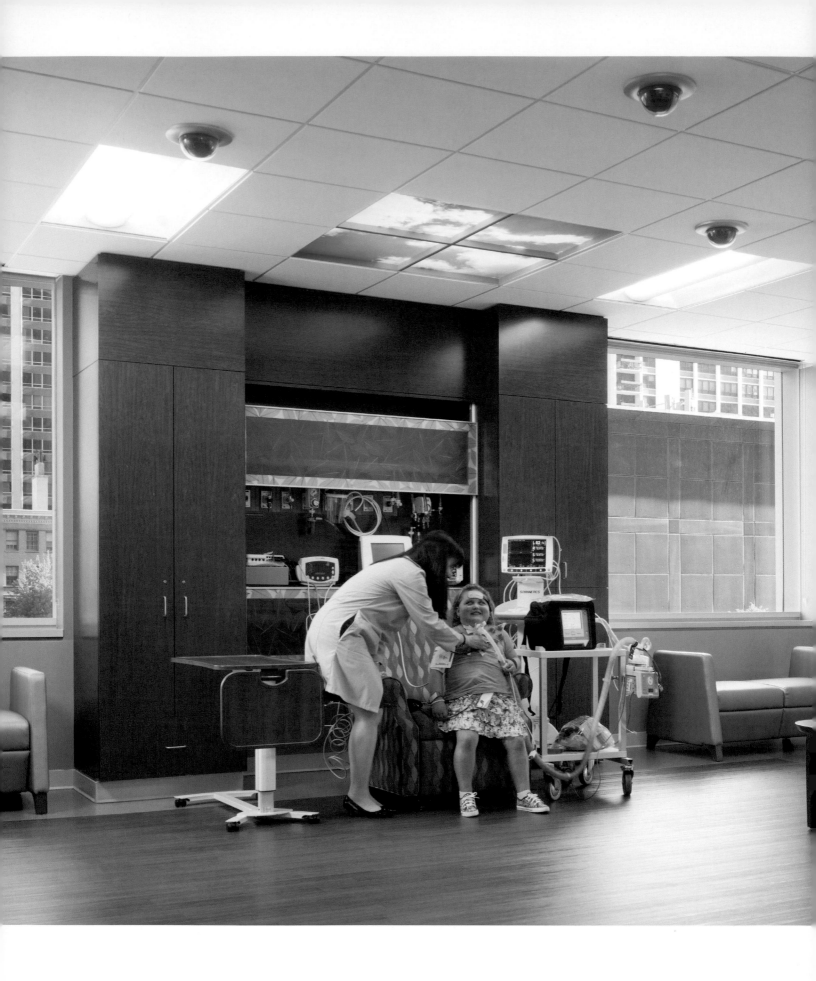

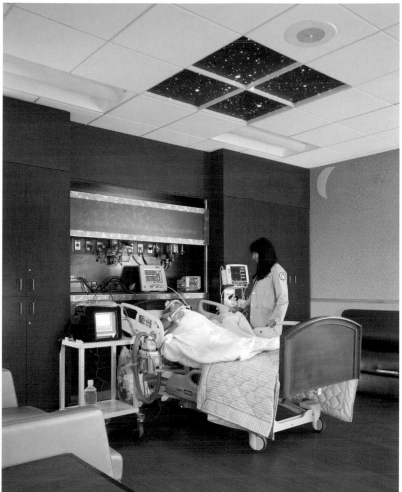

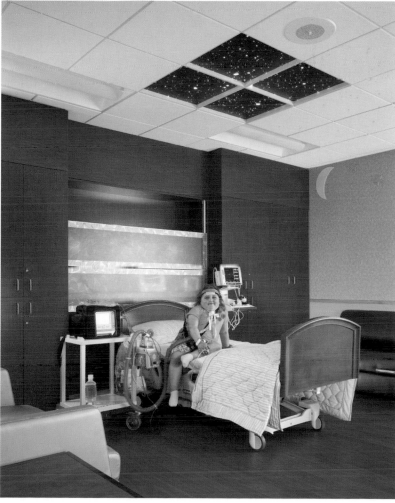

Celebrations

With thousands of diverse stakeholders impacted by and invested in the mission of this hospital, every milestone was an opportunity to celebrate.

The groundbreaking ceremony in 2008 formally began the journey. More than a thousand guests celebrated with performances from children and inspiring speeches. A few months later, the *Heroes For Life*: Campaign for Ann & Robert H. Lurie Children's Hospital of Chicago officially launched in September at an event at Northerly Island.

Some celebrations were just for hospital staff and physicians. Moving to the new hospital was a significant change for them, and celebrations were held to educate and engage them in the creation of the new hospital. They participated in town hall meetings, a contest to name the tower cranes, a celebration on-site when the building foundation hit its lowest point, several opening events to show their families their new workspace, and a closing ceremony at Children's Memorial Hospital to say goodbye.

The Topping Off ceremony was held on a cold Chicago evening in December 2009. The ceremonial final beam had spent the previous week in the lobby of the old hospital so staff, physicians, and families could sign it. That night, participants drank hot chocolate and watched as the ceremonial final beam, adorned with an evergreen tree and white roses, was raised 387 feet high in front of a color light show.

As the opening of the hospital approached in 2012, more than 15,000 people previewed the hospital during 20 events in 8 weeks. The opening events began with a fundraising Preview Gala that featured Harry Connick, Jr. and Sarah Jessica Parker. And to help celebrate the hospital's new location, a "Move for the Kids" 5K run/walk began at Children's Memorial in Lincoln Park and ended at Lurie Children's in Streeterville. A ribbon-cutting featured hospital patients, board and hospital leaders, donors, and dignitaries from across the State.

Foundation President Thomas J. Sullivan, Bruce Komiske, Jack Crocker, Ann Lurie, and Medical Center President and CEO Patrick M. Magoon

Transformational donor Ann Lurie greeted by children at groundbreaking ceremony

Campaign Public Launch Event

"Building Up From Here" event

Ann Lurie, Chicago Mayor Richard M. and Maggie Daley at Topping Off event

Ribbon Cutting and Other Celebrations

Sarah Jessica Parker, Ann Lurie, and Chicago Mayor Rahm Emanuel

Lovie and Mary Ann Smith, Larsa and Scottie Pippen

Chris and Anne Reyes

June 9, 2012 – Move Day

3.5 miles. 127 children. 14 hours. 27 ambulances.

After three years of planning, the Incident Command Centers at Children's Memorial and Lurie Children's opened at 4 a.m. on June 9, 2012. City of Chicago personnel were closing down Fullerton Avenue and traffic control aides were gathering for a final briefing before heading to their posts.

The hospital's clinical and family services teams had fully prepared each child and his or her family for the move. And from 6 a.m. until 8 p.m., one by one, each child was safely moved to the new hospital.

Clinical leaders had spent months preparing for what kinds of service and personnel would be needed for children based on a wide range of diagnoses and severity. They had conducted several "mock move" drills and knew they were ready. The hospital participated in dozens of meetings convened by the City of Chicago's Office of Emergency Management Communications to ensure that police and traffic control officers were located where they were needed and all other City agencies were prepared for the move.

Almost every hospital employee and physician was on hand. While most were providing care or assisting in the transport, some were serving as volunteers to provide wayfinding assistance to paramedics and others were cleaning off equipment as it arrived to get it to patients as fast as possible. The hospital's Founders' Board played a key role on move day. Throughout the day, 75 volunteers in bright red aprons enthusiastically managed the Welcome Center for families.

From day one of the move-planning process, patient safety was the hospital's top priority. When the last patient arrived safely at Lurie Children's and the door to Children's Memorial was ceremoniously locked, it was clear that the mission had been accomplished and a 130-year legacy was successfully transitioned to its new home.

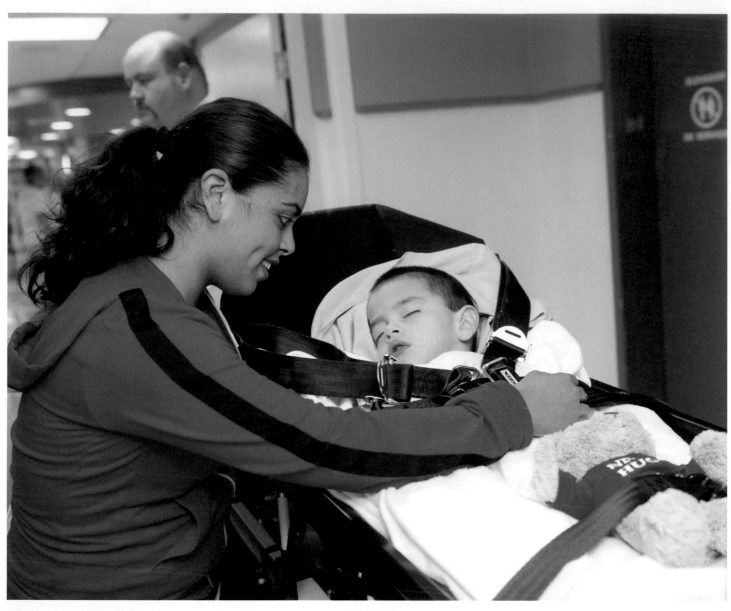

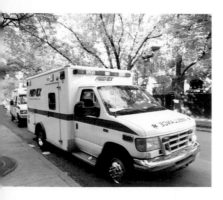

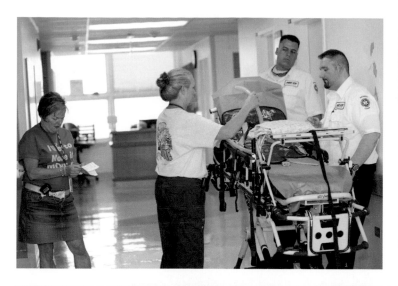

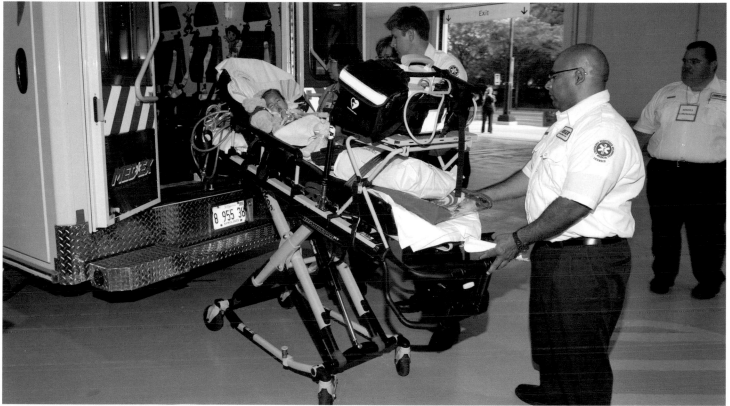

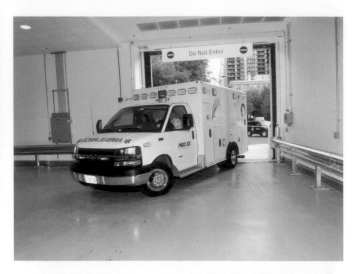

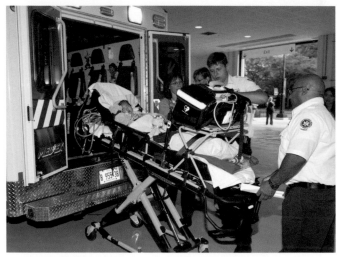

Founders' Board outgoing President Sarah Baine and incoming President Lauren Gorter

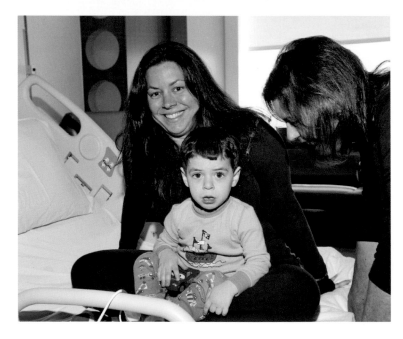

Facts and Figures

- Opened June 9, 2012 at 225 East Chicago Avenue on the campus of Northwestern University Feinberg School of Medicine

- Ranked in top 10 nationally for "Best Children's Hospitals" by *US News & World Report*

- Named for philanthropist and former pediatric nurse Ann Lurie and her late husband, Robert, in recognition of her $100 million gift

- Licensed for 288 beds and all private rooms; flexible design will enable significant bed expansion when necessary

- 23 stories and 1.25 million square feet with a total project cost of $840 million ($75 million under budget)

- Enhanced amenities for families include in-room showers, wireless internet access, on-demand in-room food service, and shared kitchen, dining, and respite spaces

- State-of-the-art rooftop heliport to receive the region's most critically ill and injured children

- Second floor emergency department includes trauma/procedure rooms, diagnostic radiology rooms, and a dedicated CT scanner

- 21 operating/procedure rooms equipped for minimally invasive surgery

- Unique pediatric cardiac care unit in which cardiology and cardiovascular surgery patients can stay from admission to discharge

- New clinical research center to expedite discoveries from the lab to the patient bedside

- Sustainable facility that will qualify for LEED Gold certification

Project Team

A special thanks to our key contractors and subcontractors who partnered with the Lurie Children's team to create the hospital.

Architects ZGF Architects LLP, Solomon Cordwell Buenz, Anderson Mikos Architects, Ltd

Construction Manager Mortenson / Power, joint venture

Program Management ARCADIS

M / E / P Engineer / Lighting Design Affiliated Engineers Inc.

Structural Engineer Magnusson Klemencic Associates

Civil Engineer V3 Companies

IT Consultant Lassen Associates, Inc.

Medical Equipment Planning Walsh Consulting Group

Wayfinding / Signage / Donor Recognition Mitchell Associates

Landscape Architect CYLA Design Associates, Inc.

Crown Sky Garden Design Mikyoung Kim Design

Materials Management / Vertical Transportation Lerch Bates

Commissioning SSR Cx / CCI

Transition Planning Kurt Salmon Associates / Balfour Resource Group

Medical Programming Kurt Salmon Associates

Fundraising Campaign Success

Heroes for Life: Campaign for Ann & Robert H. Lurie Children's Hospital of Chicago was the most ambitious fundraising initiative in the history of the hospital and one of the nation's most successful campaigns on behalf of children's health. The creation of Lurie Children's ushered in a new era in pediatric medicine and research for children and families in Chicago and beyond.

Between 2004 and 2012, more than 250,000 donors gave an aggregate total of $675 million to create the 23-story, state-of-the-art Ann & Robert H. Lurie Children's Hospital of Chicago, and provide the most advanced healthcare for children in Chicago and beyond, recruit and retain the best specialists, more effectively train the next generation of pediatric experts and enhance the hospital's ability to search for causes and innovative cures for pediatric illness and injury. Lurie Children's location on the campus of Northwestern University Feinberg School of Medicine,

its adjacency to Prentice Women's Hospital, and its close proximity to Northwestern Memorial Hospital and the Rehabilitation Institute of Chicago have led to the formation of a nucleus of world-class medical and research excellence.

The success of the *Heroes for Life* campaign was made possible through an extraordinary group of volunteer leaders who were instrumental in championing and guiding the fundraising initiative in the community. Their names will forever be associated with this great legacy to the city of Chicago. We are most grateful to:

Honorary Campaign Chairs	Campaign Chairs
Lester Crown	Paula H. Crown
Ann Lurie	Daniel J. Hennessy
Penny S. Pritzker	Robert S. Murley
Andrew J. McKenna	J. Christopher Reyes

From left: Daniel J. Hennessy, Lester Crown, Medical Center President and CEO Patrick Magoon, Ann Lurie, J. Christopher Reyes, Robert S. Murley, Paula H. Crown, Andrew J. McKenna, and Foundation President Thomas J. Sullivan

Acknowledgements

Special thanks to those who helped make this book a reality:

Patrick Magoon

Ken Labok

Mary Kate Daly

Colin Harding

Debra Weese-Mayer, MD

Alice Archabal

Erin Shields

Kathleen Keenan

Photo credits